T0039797

TRUMPET
101 BROADWAY SONGS

Available for
FLUTE, CLARINET, ALTO SAX, TENOR SAX, TRUMPET,
HORN, TROMBONE, VIOLIN, VIOLA, CELLO

ISBN 978-1-4950-5250-7

Visit Hal Leonard Online at
www.halleonard.com

Contact us:
Hal Leonard
7777 West Bluemound Road
Milwaukee, WI 53213
Email: info@halleonard.com

In Europe, contact:
Hal Leonard Europe Limited
42 Wigmore Street
Marylebone, London, W1U 2RN
Email: info@halleonardeurope.com

In Australia, contact:
Hal Leonard Australia Pty. Ltd.
4 Lentara Court
Cheltenham, Victoria, 3192 Australia
Email: info@halleonard.com.au

CONTENTS

ALL I ASK OF YOU

from THE PHANTOM OF THE OPERA

TRUMPET

Music by ANDREW LLOYD WEBBER
Lyrics by CHARLES HART
Additional Lyrics by RICHARD STILGOE

ANY DREAM WILL DO

from JOSEPH AND THE AMAZING TECHNICOLOR® DREAMCOAT

TRUMPET

Music by ANDREW LLOYD WEBBER
Lyrics by TIM RICE

ANYTHING YOU CAN DO

from the Stage Production ANNIE GET YOUR GUN

TRUMPET

Words and Music by
IRVING BERLIN

AS IF WE NEVER SAID GOODBYE

from SUNSET BOULEVARD

TRUMPET

Music by ANDREW LLOYD WEBBER
Lyrics by DON BLACK and CHRISTOPHER HAMPTON,
with contributions by AMY POWERS

AS LONG AS HE NEEDS ME

from the Broadway Musical OLIVER!

TRUMPET

Words and Music by
LIONEL BART

BALI HA'I
from SOUTH PACIFIC

TRUMPET

Lyrics by OSCAR HAMMERSTEIN II
Music by RICHARD RODGERS

BAUBLES, BANGLES AND BEADS

from KISMET

TRUMPET

Words and Music by ROBERT WRIGHT
and GEORGE FORREST
(Music Based on Themes of A. BORODIN)

BROTHERHOOD OF MAN
from HOW TO SUCCEED IN BUSINESS WITHOUT REALLY TRYING

TRUMPET

By FRANK LOESSER

CABARET
from the Musical CABARET

TRUMPET

Words by FRED EBB
Music by JOHN KANDER

CAN'T TAKE MY EYES OFF OF YOU

featured in JERSEY BOYS

TRUMPET

Words and Music by BOB CREWE
and BOB GAUDIO

CIRCLE OF LIFE

Disney Presents THE LION KING: THE BROADWAY MUSICAL

TRUMPET

Music by ELTON JOHN
Lyrics by TIM RICE

Moderately, with an African beat

CLIMB EV'RY MOUNTAIN
from THE SOUND OF MUSIC

TRUMPET

Lyrics by OSCAR HAMMERSTEIN II
Music by RICHARD RODGERS

Majestically

CLOSE EVERY DOOR

from JOSEPH AND THE AMAZING TECHNICOLOR® DREAMCOAT

Music by ANDREW LLOYD WEBBER
Lyrics by TIM RICE

Moderately, expressively

DANCING QUEEN

from MAMMA MIA!

TRUMPET

Words and Music by BENNY ANDERSSON,
BJÖRN ULVAEUS and STIG ANDERSON

DEFYING GRAVITY
from the Broadway Musical WICKED

TRUMPET

Music and Lyrics by
STEPHEN SCHWARTZ

Tempo I

DO-RE-MI
from THE SOUND OF MUSIC

TRUMPET

Lyrics by OSCAR HAMMERSTEIN II
Music by RICHARD RODGERS

DO YOU HEAR THE PEOPLE SING?

from LES MISÉRABLES

TRUMPET

Music by CLAUDE-MICHEL SCHÖNBERG
Lyrics by ALAIN BOUBLIL, JEAN-MARC NATEL
and HERBERT KRETZMER

DON'T CRY FOR ME ARGENTINA
from EVITA

TRUMPET

Words by TIM RICE
Music by ANDREW LLOYD WEBBER

EASTER PARADE

from AS THOUSANDS CHEER

TRUMPET

Words and Music by
IRVING BERLIN

EDELWEISS
from THE SOUND OF MUSIC

TRUMPET

Lyrics by OSCAR HAMMERSTEIN II
Music by RICHARD RODGERS

Slowly, with expression

EVERYTHING'S ALRIGHT
from JESUS CHRIST SUPERSTAR

TRUMPET

Words by TIM RICE
Music by ANDREW LLOYD WEBBER

A FOGGY DAY (IN LONDON TOWN)

from A DAMSEL IN DISTRESS

TRUMPET

Music and Lyrics by GEORGE GERSHWIN
and IRA GERSHWIN

GETTING TO KNOW YOU

from THE KING AND I

TRUMPET

Lyrics by OSCAR HAMMERSTEIN II
Music by RICHARD RODGERS

FRIEND LIKE ME
(Stageplay Version)
from the Walt Disney Stageplay ALADDIN

TRUMPET

Music by ALAN MENKEN
Lyrics by HOWARD ASHMAN
and STEPHEN SCHWARTZ

GUYS AND DOLLS

from GUYS AND DOLLS

TRUMPET

By FRANK LOESSER

HELLO, DOLLY!

from HELLO, DOLLY!

TRUMPET

Music and Lyric by
JERRY HERMAN

HOME

from Walt Disney's BEAUTY AND THE BEAST: THE BROADWAY MUSICAL

TRUMPET

Music by ALAN MENKEN
Lyrics by TIM RICE

HOW ARE THINGS IN GLOCCA MORRA

from FINIAN'S RAINBOW

TRUMPET

Words by E.Y. "YIP" HARBURG
Music by BURTON LANE

I BELIEVE IN YOU

from HOW TO SUCCEED IN BUSINESS WITHOUT REALLY TRYING

TRUMPET

By FRANK LOESSER

I DON'T KNOW HOW TO LOVE HIM

from JESUS CHRIST SUPERSTAR

TRUMPET

Words by TIM RICE
Music by ANDREW LLOYD WEBBER

Slowly, expressively

I DREAMED A DREAM
from LES MISÉRABLES

TRUMPET

Music by CLAUDE-MICHEL SCHÖNBERG
Lyrics by ALAIN BOUBLIL, JEAN-MARC NATEL
and HERBERT KRETZMER

Moderately slow

I GOT PLENTY O' NUTTIN'

from PORGY AND BESS ®

TRUMPET

Music and Lyrics by GEORGE GERSHWIN,
DuBOSE and DORTHY HEYWARD
and IRA GERSHWIN

I WHISTLE A HAPPY TUNE

from THE KING AND I

TRUMPET

Lyrics by OSCAR HAMMERSTEIN II
Music by RICHARD RODGERS

I'VE NEVER BEEN IN LOVE BEFORE

from GUYS AND DOLLS

TRUMPET

By FRANK LOESSER

IF I LOVED YOU

from CAROUSEL

TRUMPET

Lyrics by OSCAR HAMMERSTEIN II
Music by RICHARD RODGERS

IF I WERE A BELL

from GUYS AND DOLLS

TRUMPET

By FRANK LOESSER

IF I WERE A RICH MAN
from the Musical FIDDLER ON THE ROOF

TRUMPET

Words by SHELDON HARNICK
Music by JERRY BOCK

THE IMPOSSIBLE DREAM
(The Quest)
from MAN OF LA MANCHA

Lyric by JOE DARION
Music by MITCH LEIGH

IT AIN'T NECESSARILY SO

from PORGY AND BESS®

TRUMPET

Music and Lyrics by GEORGE GERSHWIN,
DuBOSE and DOROTHY HEYWARD
and IRA GERSHWIN

THE LADY IS A TRAMP

from BABES IN ARMS

TRUMPET

Words by LORENZ HART
Music by RICHARD RODGERS

THE LAST NIGHT OF THE WORLD

from MISS SAIGON

TRUMPET

Music by CLAUDE-MICHEL SCHÖNBERG
Lyrics by ALAIN BOUBLIL and RICHARD MALTBY JR.
Adapted from original French Lyrics by ALAIN BOUBLIL

LET'S CALL THE WHOLE THING OFF
from SHALL WE DANCE

TRUMPET

Music and Lyrics by GEORGE GERSHWIN
and IRA GERSHWIN

LOVE IS HERE TO STAY

from GOLDWYN FOLLIES

TRUMPET

Music and Lyrics by GEORGE GERSHWIN
and IRA GERSHWIN

LOVE ME OR LEAVE ME

from WHOOPEE!

TRUMPET

Lyrics by GUS KAHN
Music by WALTER DONALDSON

LOVE WALKED IN
from GOLDWYN FOLLIES

TRUMPET

Music and Lyrics by GEORGE GERSHWIN
and IRA GERSHWIN

LUCK BE A LADY
from GUYS AND DOLLS

TRUMPET

By FRANK LOESSER

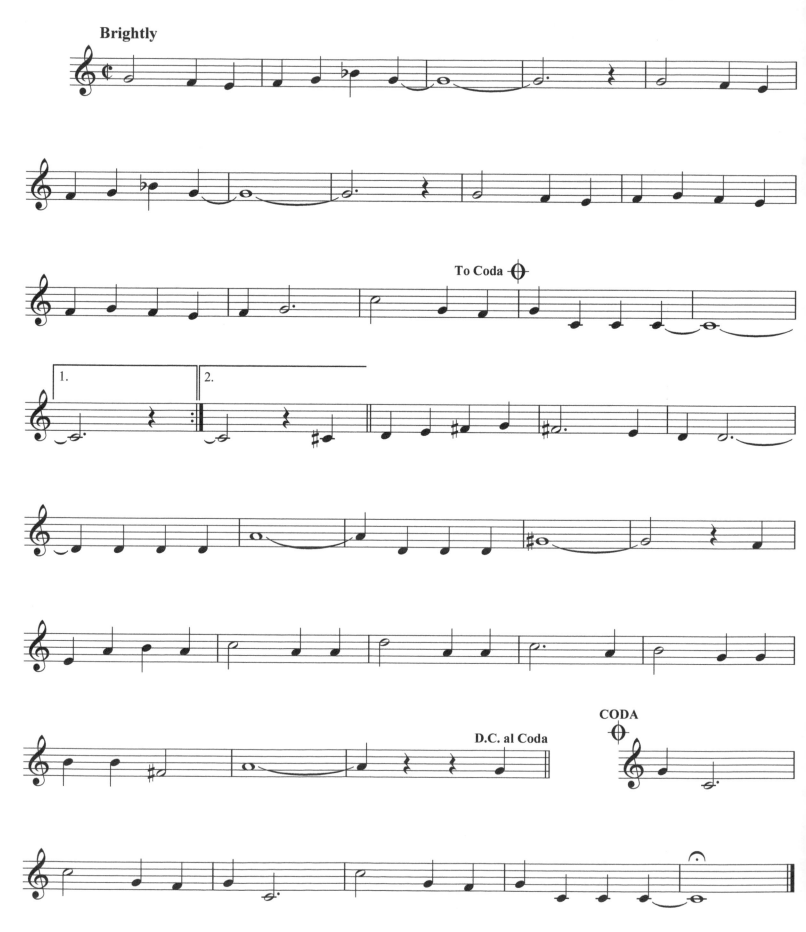

MAKIN' WHOOPEE!

from WHOOPEE!

TRUMPET

Lyrics by GUS KAHN
Music by WALTER DONALDSON

MAME
from MAME

TRUMPET

Music and Lyric by
JERRY HERMAN

MAMMA MIA
from MAMMA MIA!

TRUMPET

Words and Music by BENNY ANDERSSON,
BJÖRN ULVAEUS and STIG ANDERSON

MATCHMAKER
from the Musical FIDDLER ON THE ROOF

Words by SHELDON HARNICK
Music by JERRY BOCK

TRUMPET

MAYBE

from the Musical Production ANNIE

Lyric by MARTIN CHARNIN
Music by CHARLES STROUSE

TRUMPET

MEMORY
from CATS

TRUMPET

Music by ANDREW LLOYD WEBBER
Text by TREVOR NUNN after T.S. ELIOT

THE MUSIC OF THE NIGHT

from THE PHANTOM OF THE OPERA

TRUMPET

Music by ANDREW LLOYD WEBBER
Lyrics by CHARLES HART
Additional Lyrics by RICHARD STILGOE

MY FAVORITE THINGS
from THE SOUND OF MUSIC

TRUMPET

Lyrics by OSCAR HAMMERSTEIN II
Music by RICHARD RODGERS

Lively, with spirit

NICE WORK IF YOU CAN GET IT

from A DAMSEL IN DISTRESS

TRUMPET

Music and Lyrics by GEORGE GERSHWIN
and IRA GERSWIN

OH, WHAT A BEAUTIFUL MORNIN'

from OKLAHOMA!

TRUMPET

Lyrics by OSCAR HAMMERSTEIN II
Music by RICHARD RODGERS

Bright Waltz

OKLAHOMA
from OKLAHOMA!

TRUMPET

Lyrics by OSCAR HAMMERSTEIN II
Music by RICHARD RODGERS

OL' MAN RIVER
from SHOW BOAT

TRUMPET

Lyrics by OSCAR HAMMERSTEIN II
Music by JEROME KERN

OLD DEVIL MOON

from FINIAN'S RAINBOW

TRUMPET

Words by E.Y. "YIP" HARBURG
Music by BURTON LANE

ON MY OWN
from LES MISÉRABLES

TRUMPET

Music by CLAUDE-MICHEL SCHÖNBERG
Lyrics by ALAIN BOUBLIL, JEAN-MARC NATEL,
HERBERT KRETZMER, JOHN CAIRD
and TREVOR NUNN

Moderately slow

ONCE IN A LIFETIME

from the Musical Production STOP THE WORLD—I WANT TO GET OFF

TRUMPET

Words and Music by LESLIE BRICUSSE
and ANTHONY NEWLEY

ONCE IN LOVE WITH AMY
from WHERE'S CHARLEY?

TRUMPET

By FRANK LOESSER

ONE

from A CHORUS LINE

TRUMPET

Music by MARVIN HAMLISCH
Lyric by EDWARD KLEBAN

PEOPLE WILL SAY WE'RE IN LOVE

from OKLAHOMA!

TRUMPET

Lyrics by OSCAR HAMMERSTEIN II
Music by RICHARD RODGERS

THE PHANTOM OF THE OPERA
from THE PHANTOM OF THE OPERA

Music by ANDREW LLOYD WEBBER
Lyrics by CHARLES HART
Additional Lyrics by RICHARD STILGOE
and MIKE BATT

TRUMPET

Moderately fast

POPULAR
from the Broadway Musical WICKED

TRUMPET

Music and Lyrics by
STEPHEN SCHWARTZ

SEASONS OF LOVE
from RENT

TRUMPET

Words and Music by
JONATHAN LARSON

Moderately

SEND IN THE CLOWNS
from the Musical A LITTLE NIGHT MUSIC

TRUMPET

Words and Music by
STEPHEN SONDHEIM

SEVENTY SIX TROMBONES
from Meredith Willson's THE MUSIC MAN

TRUMPET

By MEREDITH WILLSON

SHALL WE DANCE?

from THE KING AND I

TRUMPET

Lyrics by OSCAR HAMMERSTEIN II
Music by RICHARD RODGERS

SHE LOVES ME

from SHE LOVES ME

TRUMPET

Words by SHELDON HARNICK
Music by JERRY BOCK

SHERRY
featured in JERSEY BOYS

TRUMPET

Words and Music by
BOB GAUDIO

SOME ENCHANTED EVENING

from SOUTH PACIFIC

TRUMPET

Lyrics by OSCAR HAMMERSTEIN II
Music by RICHARD RODGERS

SUMMERTIME

from PORGY AND BESS®

TRUMPET

Music and Lyrics by GEORGE GERSHWIN,
DuBOSE and DOROTHY HEYWARD
and IRA GERSHWIN

SUNRISE, SUNSET

from the Musical FIDDLER ON THE ROOF

TRUMPET

Words by SHELDON HARNICK
Music by JERRY BOCK

SUPERSTAR
from JESUS CHRIST SUPERSTAR

TRUMPET

Words by TIM RICE
Music by ANDREW LLOYD WEBBER

THE SURREY WITH THE FRINGE ON TOP

from OKLAHOMA!

TRUMPET

Lyrics by OSCAR HAMMERSTEIN II
Music by RICHARD RODGERS

THE SWEETEST SOUNDS
from NO STRINGS

TRUMPET

Lyrics and Music by
RICHARD RODGERS

THERE'S NO BUSINESS LIKE SHOW BUSINESS

from the Stage Production ANNIE GET YOUR GUN

TRUMPET

Words and Music by
IRVING BERLIN

THEY ALL LAUGHED

from SHALL WE DANCE

TRUMPET

Music and Lyrics by GEORGE GERSHWIN
and IRA GERSHWIN

THEY CAN'T TAKE THAT AWAY FROM ME

from SHALL WE DANCE

TRUMPET

Music and Lyrics by GEORGE GERSHWIN
and IRA GERSHWIN

THINK OF ME
from THE PHANTOM OF THE OPERA

TRUMPET

Music by ANDREW LLOYD WEBBER
Lyrics by CHARLES HART
Additional Lyrics by RICHARD STILGOE

THIS IS THE MOMENT

from JEKYLL & HYDE

TRUMPET

Words and Music by LESLIE BRICUSSE
and FRANK WILDHORN

THIS NEARLY WAS MINE

from SOUTH PACIFIC

TRUMPET

Lyrics by OSCAR HAMMERSTEIN II
Music by RICHARD RODGERS

TILL THERE WAS YOU

from Meredith Willson's THE MUSIC MAN

TRUMPET

By MEREDITH WILLSON

TOMORROW
from the Musical Production ANNIE

TRUMPET

Lyric by MARTIN CHARNIN
Music by CHARLES STROUSE

WALK LIKE A MAN

featured in JERSEY BOYS

TRUMPET

Words and Music by BOB CREWE
and BOB GAUDIO

UNUSUAL WAY

from NINE

TRUMPET

Music and Lyrics by
MAURY YESTON

WHAT I DID FOR LOVE

from A CHORUS LINE

TRUMPET

Music by MARVIN HAMLISCH
Lyric by EDWARD KLEBAN

WHAT KIND OF FOOL AM I?

from the Musical Production STOP THE WORLD—I WANT TO GET OFF

TRUMPET

Words and Music by LESLIE BRICUSSE
and ANTHONY NEWLEY

WHERE IS LOVE?

from the Broadway Musical OLIVER!

TRUMPET

Words and Music by
LIONEL BART

WHO CAN I TURN TO
(When Nobody Needs Me)
from THE ROAR OF THE GREASEPAINT—THE SMELL OF THE CROWD

Words and Music by LESLIE BRICUSSE
and ANTHONY NEWLEY

TRUMPET

A WHOLE NEW WORLD

from the Walt Disney Stageplay ALADDIN

TRUMPET

Music by ALAN MENKEN
Lyrics by TIM RICE

WILL YOU LOVE ME TOMORROW
(Will You Still Love Me Tomorrow)
from BEAUTIFUL

Words and Music by GERRY GOFFIN
and CAROLE KING

TRUMPET

WITH ONE LOOK
from SUNSET BOULEVARD

TRUMPET

Music by ANDREW LLOYD WEBBER
Lyrics by DON BLACK and CHRISTOPHER HAMPTON,
with contributions by AMY POWERS

WRITTEN IN THE STARS

from Elton John and Tim Rice's AIDA

Music by ELTON JOHN
Lyrics by TIM RICE

TRUMPET

YOU RULE MY WORLD
from THE FULL MONTY

TRUMPET

Words and Music by
DAVID YAZBEK

YOU'LL NEVER WALK ALONE

from CAROUSEL

TRUMPET

Lyrics by OSCAR HAMMERSTEIN II
Music by RICHARD RODGERS

Moderately

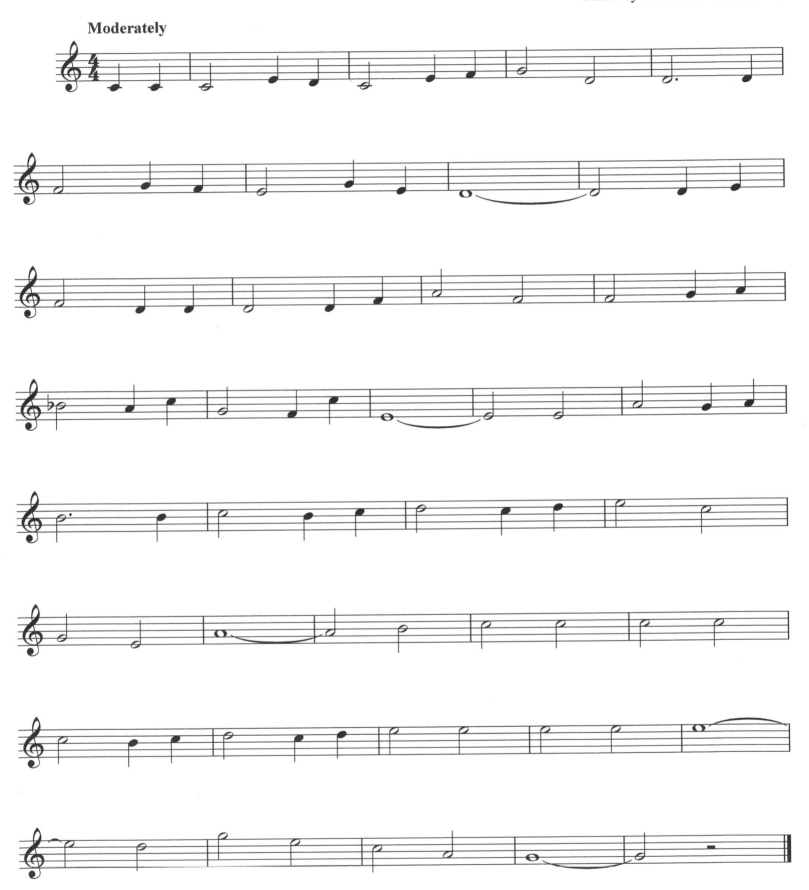

YOU'LL BE IN MY HEART

Disney Presents TARZAN The Broadway Musical

TRUMPET

Words and Music by
PHIL COLLINS

D.S. al Coda

CODA

YOU'VE GOT A FRIEND

from BEAUTIFUL

TRUMPET

Words and Music by
CAROLE KING

Moderately

YOUNGER THAN SPRINGTIME
from SOUTH PACIFIC

TRUMPET

Lyrics by OSCAR HAMMERSTEIN II
Music by RICHARD RODGERS